THIS BOOK BELONGS TO:

Thank you so much for purchasing one of my "bold & easy" coloring books! I hope you have as much fun coloring the designs as I did drawing them. I appreciate all the support so much!

♡ megan

MeganMilesArt.com

P.S. THE PAGES ARE SINGLE-SIDED TO PREVENT MARKER BLEED BUT YOU STILL NEED TO PUT EXTRA PAPER OR CARD STOCK UNDER IT.

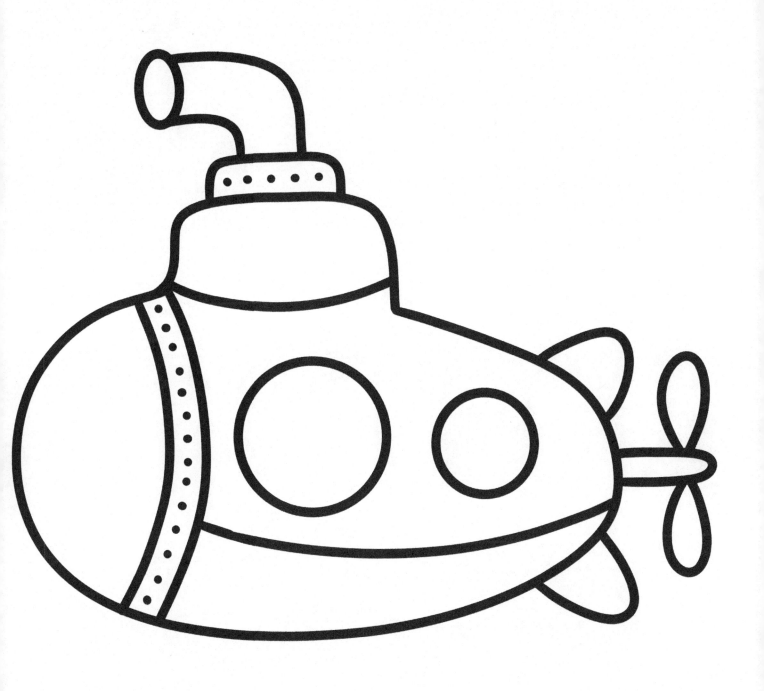

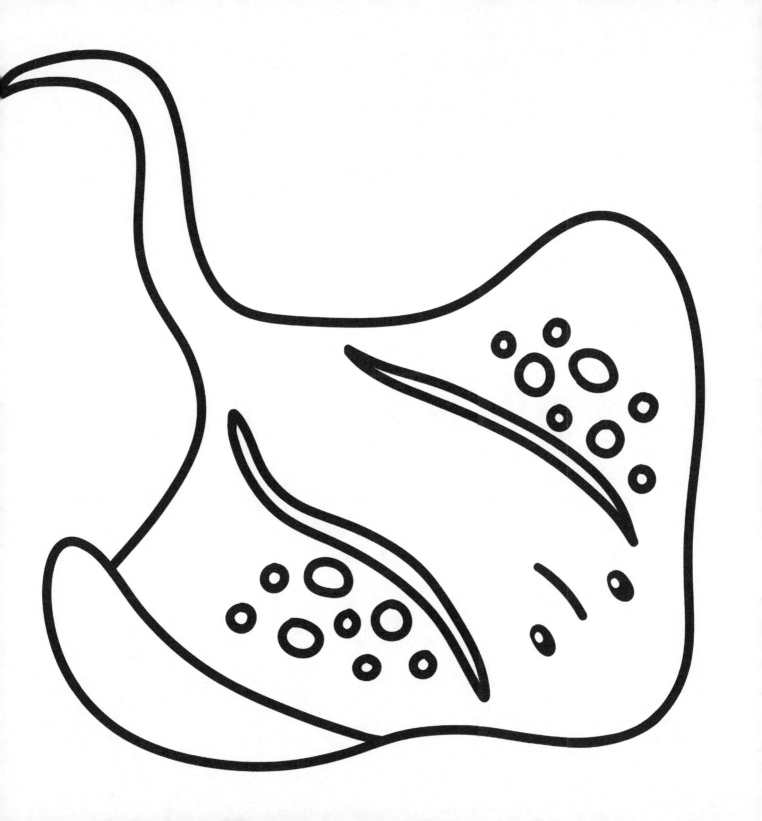

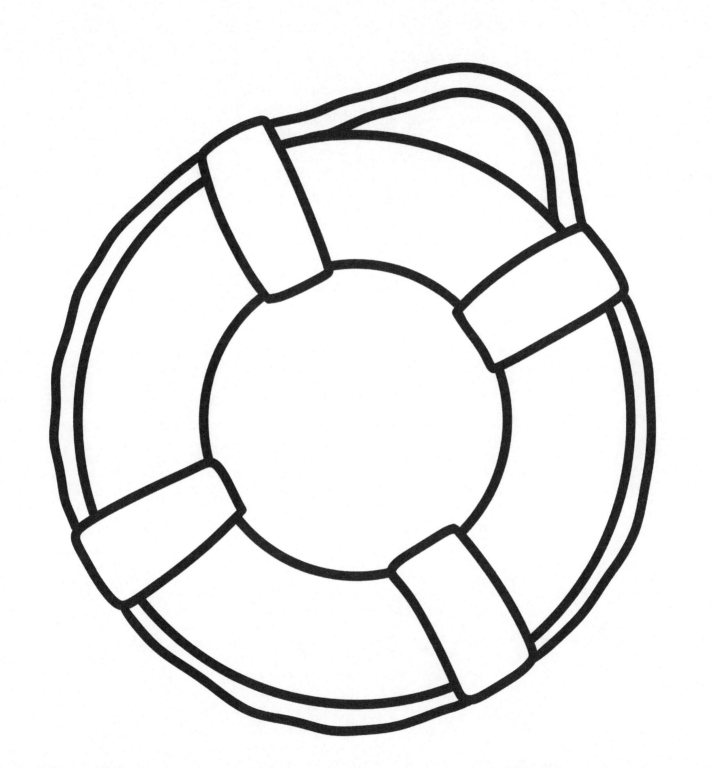

Extra paper for testing markers or to put behind
the page you're coloring to prevent bleeding

Extra paper for testing markers or to put behind
the page you're coloring to prevent bleeding

Extra paper for testing markers or to put behind
the page you're coloring to prevent bleeding

Made in the USA
Las Vegas, NV
25 April 2024

89118662R00050